WINNING PEOPLE OVER

"From Skepticism To Support"

ETHAN YODER

COPYRIGHT

Copyright ©2023 [Ethan Yoder]. All rights reserved. No part of this publication may be reproduced, distributed, or transmitted in any form or by any means, including photocopying, recording, or other electronic or mechanical methods, without the prior written permission of the copyright holder, except in the case of brief quotations embodied in critical reviews and certain other noncommercial uses permitted.

CONTENTS

Introduction

In the dimly lit conference room in 1999, I stood alone at the front, my heart pounding with a mixture of excitement and nervous anticipation. The slide projector hummed softly in the background, casting a soft glow on the blank screen behind me. A sea of skeptical faces stared back, each one a testament to the challenge I was about to face.

As a young, inexperienced speaker, the odds were stacked against me. My audience, a diverse and discerning crowd, had gathered for a conference on innovation and leadership. They came for wisdom, for inspiration, and, above all, to be won over by ideas worth their time.

The murmurs in the crowd hinted at their skepticism. Whispers of doubt danced in the air. I was the underdog, the unknown voice in a sea of established thought leaders. And as the minutes ticked away, it seemed that the spotlight was my only ally, casting shadows where I stood.

I had been invited to speak at one of the most prestigious industry events of the year. It was an opportunity that could propel my career to new heights, but as I looked out at the audience of experts, decision-makers, and competitors, doubt gnawed at the edges of my confidence.

As I began my presentation, I could feel the weight of their expectations pressing down on me. The room was silent, except for the soft click of the remote control as I advanced the slides. My words flowed, and the data I presented was strong, but it was clear that something was missing. I needed to connect with these individuals on a deeper level, to make them believe in not just the information I was sharing but in me as a communicator and a leader.

Then, I remembered a story. A story from my own experiences, one that perfectly illustrated the core message of my presentation. It was a tale of overcoming challenges, of resilience, and of innovation, and it had the potential to resonate with everyone in that room.

With a deep breath, I paused the presentation and began to share my story.

As I spoke, I watched the room transform. Skepticism turned into curiosity, and curious glances turned into focused attention. The audience leaned in, captivated by the narrative I was weaving.

The room grew hushed, and I began. I spoke not as an expert but as a fellow traveler on the road of innovation, a seeker of better ways and fresh perspectives. I recounted failures and, from those ashes, the spark of insight that had fueled my passion.

As the narrative unfolded, I could feel the audience's attention shift. The skepticism transformed into curiosity. Heads nodded in understanding, smiles broke through the initial reserve, and palpable energy surged in the room. My audience was being won over, not by a polished facade of authority but by the authenticity of the journey I had undertaken.

My heart no longer pounded with nervousness but with the thrill of connection. In that moment, I wasn't just presenting data; I was sharing a piece of myself. The room came alive with energy, and by the time I concluded, I could see it in their eyes—I had won them over.

In those moments, I understood the power of relatability, the strength of vulnerability, and the potential for genuine connection through storytelling. The audience wasn't merely won over; they had become allies in a shared quest for innovation. It was a reminder that, in the world of ideas, the most compelling victories are not won through force but through the subtle art of winning hearts and minds.

The Q&A session that followed was vibrant, filled with insightful questions and genuine interest. People approached me during the break, eager to discuss ideas and partnerships. I had not only delivered a compelling presentation, but I had connected with my audience on a personal level, and it had made all the difference.

In the pages that follow, I'll share the strategies and insights that allowed me to win over that tough crowd and how you can do the same. Whether it's in the boardroom, on the stage, or in your everyday interactions, the art of persuasion and connection is a powerful tool that can open doors and create opportunities beyond your wildest dreams.

The Power of Persuasion

The influential ability is a convincing and persuasive power that can be tackled in different parts of life, from individual connections to business and influential positions. It includes the capacity to persuade and influence others to embrace a specific perspective, simply decide, or make explicit moves. Successful influence draws upon a scope of procedures and abilities, like clear and enticing correspondence, the introduction of undeniable proof or contentions, grasping the necessities and inspirations of your crowd, and the foundation of trust and compatibility.

The craft of influence isn't about control yet rather the specialty of truly and morally directing others to see the worth or advantage in what you propose. By figuring out human brain science, profound triggers, and mental inclinations, you can turn into a more influential communicator.

Whether you are trying to impact your partners, arrange an arrangement, or rouse change, dominating the influential ability can be a significant device for accomplishing your objectives and building significant associations. In this investigation, we will dig into the brain research, techniques, and moral contemplations behind successful influence to assist you with turning into an additional powerful and compelling person.

Why Winning People Over Matters

Winning people over is a crucial expertise with broad ramifications, as it holds importance in different parts of life. The capacity to associate, convince, and gain the trust of others is fundamental because of multiple factors.

First and foremost, building connections is at the center of human association.

The associations we lay out with companions, family, partners, and colleagues shape our profound prosperity and emotionally supportive networks. Winning people over makes us ready to support these associations, making an organization of people who comprehend, appreciate, and stand by us.

Powerful correspondence is another key explanation. At the point when people are prevailed upon, they are bound to listen mindfully and be open to what we need to say. This works with the trading of thoughts, data, and sentiments, prompting useful discourse and a decrease in false impressions and clashes.

Impact and administration are intently attached to the capacity to prevail upon people. Pioneers who can convince, propel, and gain the trust of their groups or adherents will generally accomplish more huge results. Their direction is regarded, and their vision is embraced, bringing about the aggregate accomplishment of objectives.

Winning people over is especially significant in exchanges and compromise. Whether in transactions, individual debates, or worldwide discretion, the ability to convince others and settle on something worth agreeing on is essential for accomplishing commonly helpful results.

Expertly, this ability can prompt professional success. The people who can win partners, clients, or bosses over frequently end up in beneficial positions, which can bring about advancements, extended open doors, and a positive standing inside the working environment.

Self-improvement is an intrinsic part of winning people over. It requires better tuning in, compassion, and flexibility, empowering people to work on their relational abilities and expand their perspectives.

Moreover, winning people over is significant for embracing advancement and change.

Associations and networks depend on the help and participation of their individuals to adjust to new conditions and cultivate progress. The capacity to prevail upon people can smooth the progress and energize acknowledgment of clever thoughts and techniques.

On a more extensive scale, winning people over assumes an essential part in driving social change and local area commitment. It's an impetus for uniting people to pursue shared objectives, whether in magnanimous undertakings, political developments, or nearby drives.

At long last, there's an individual and close to home satisfaction that accompanies having the option to prevail upon people. Realizing that you have emphatically impacted and associated with others can support confidence, satisfaction, and give a significant feeling of motivation throughout everyday life.

In rundown, the capacity to prevail upon people isn't simply an important expertise; it's a foundation of compelling correspondence, initiative, and the positive progression of individual and aggregate objectives. It adds to progress, further developed connections, and a more profound feeling of satisfaction throughout everyday life.

CHAPTER 1

The Psychology Of Persuasion

The psychology of persuasion is an interesting and multifaceted field that dives into the components behind why people say "OK" to specific solicitations, thoughts, or activities. It is a basic area of study for anybody hoping to turn out to be more powerful and enticing in different parts of life, from promoting and deals to initiative and individual connections.

Key Mental Principles:

1. Reciprocity: One of the fundamental standards of persuasion is the possibility of correspondence. People will generally feel obliged to offer back when they get something.

By offering worth, help, or a little concession, you can set off a feeling of obligation in others, making them bound to conform to your solicitations.

2.   Consistency and Commitment: Individuals genuinely want to be steady with their past activities and explanations. When somebody earnestly commits a responsibility, even a little one, they are bound to finish extra, related activities. Consistency is a strong device in persuasion.

3.   Social Proof: People frequently seek others for direction in navigation. The standard of social confirmation proposes that people are bound to take on a way of behaving or conviction assuming they see others doing likewise. Tributes, surveys, and measurements can act as convincing devices.

4.   Liking: People are bound to be convinced by people they like and trust. Building compatibility and a positive relationship with your crowd can fundamentally expand your influential power.

5. Authority: People will generally follow the lead of tenable specialists or definitive figures. Exhibiting your aptitude and validity can be powerful in convincing others.

6. Scarcity: The impression of shortage or restricted accessibility can drive people to make a move. When something is viewed as uncommon or popular, people are more roused to immediately take advantage of the chance.

Mental Inclinations and Persuasion:

Mental predispositions, which are deliberate examples of deviation from standard or soundness in judgment, frequently assume a critical part in persuasion. For instance, tendency to look for predictable feedback can lead people to incline toward data that affirms their current convictions, while the mooring predisposition can impact decisions in light of an underlying snippet of data.

Understanding these predispositions is pivotal for creating convincing messages that reverberate with the manner in which people think and simply decide.

Moral Considerations:

It is vital for note that the psychology of persuasion can be utilized for both moral and dishonest purposes. While understanding these standards can upgrade your capacity to convey successfully and gain arrangement, it ought to be utilized capably and with deference for the independence and prosperity of others.

In this segment, we have presented the principal ideas of the psychology of persuasion. In resulting segments, we will investigate useful systems and utilizations of these standards in different settings to assist you with turning into a more enticing and compelling communicator.

The Science Behind Convincing Others

The specialty of persuading others is supported by the study of human direction, psychology, and correspondence. It includes a nuanced comprehension of people's thought process, feel, and answer convincing messages. The science behind persuading others isn't just about instinct yet additionally an orderly investigation of mental, emotional, and social perspectives. We should dive into a few key features:

1. Emotion versus Logic:

Viable persuasion perceives the transaction among emotion and logic in direction. Emotions can trigger speedy, instinctive choices, while logic requests thinking and proof based thinking. Capable persuasion includes an agreeable mix of emotional commitment and logical argumentation, tending to both the heart and the psyche.

2. Neuroscience of Persuasion:

Neuroscientists have caused fascinating discoveries about how our minds answer enticing messages. For example, narrating has been found to trigger the arrival of oxytocin, frequently alluded to as the "holding chemical." This hormonal response encourages trust and association with the narrator. Understanding the neurological underpinnings of persuasion can help with creating additional convincing accounts and messages.

3. Conduct Economics:

Conduct financial aspects investigates how psychological elements impact monetary choices. Ideas like misfortune revolution (the apprehension about losing something), gift impact (doling out higher worth to what we have), and exaggerated limiting (favoring quick prizes over deferred ones) all assume essential parts in affecting navigation. Talented persuaders influence these mental predispositions to poke people towards wanted decisions.

4. Psychological Triggers:

The study of persuasion uncovers different psychological triggers that can be bridled to impact choices. These triggers incorporate mental disharmony (the uneasiness brought about by holding clashing convictions), the Zeigarnik impact (the possibility that incomplete errands are better recollected), and the simple openness impact (the inclination to incline toward things experienced all the more oftentimes). By getting it and applying these psychological peculiarities, persuaders can have a strong impact.

How People Decide

Understanding how people pursue choices is the foundation of viable persuasion. Independent direction is an intricate interaction impacted by a huge number of elements, frequently extending past sanity:

1. Sane Choice Making:

Generally, direction is depicted as a sane cycle including a cautious assessment of upsides and downsides. While this model holds for specific choices, numerous decisions are influenced by mental easy routes, emotions, and predispositions, settling on the scene of choice making undeniably more complicated.

2. Framework 1 and Framework 2 Thinking:

Nobel laureate Daniel Kahneman presented the idea of Framework 1 (quick, programmed, emotional) and Framework 2 (slow, intentional, logical) thinking.

People consistently progress between these frameworks relying upon the choice's intricacy. Perceiving this duality is urgent for understanding how people process data and simply decide.

3. Heuristics:

People habitually utilize mental easy routes or heuristics to go with quick choices. These alternate routes can incidentally prompt inclinations, like the accessibility heuristic (depending on promptly accessible data) or the representativeness heuristic (making decisions in light of generalizations). Persuaders should be aware of these mental examples.

4. Prospect Theory:

The spearheading work of Kahneman and Tversky yielded the Possibility Hypothesis, which states that people will generally keep away from misfortunes more intensely than they look for identical additions.

This hypothesis highlights the meaning of outlining choices in a manner that limits apparent misfortunes or boosts apparent increases.

5. Limited Rationality:

Herbert Simon's idea of limited sanity recognizes that people have restricted mental assets and can't necessarily settle on completely objective choices. All things considered, people frequently look for "satisficing" arrangements that are "adequate" instead of ideal. This idea challenges the customary thought of totally reasonable direction.

6. The Impact of Context:

The setting where a choice is made can apply a significant impact. Little changes in how choices are introduced or the request in which decisions are offered can prompt altogether various choices. This idea, known as decision engineering, features the significance of making way for good decisions.

Understanding these elements gives the establishment a fitting convincing message to line up with the unpredictable ways people simply decide. Powerful persuaders are definitely receptive to the emotional and mental subtleties that impact decisions and utilize this information to pass on their messages and impact results in a calculated way.

Integrating these bits of knowledge into persuasion methodologies can fundamentally upgrade the capacity to persuade others, cultivating more fruitful correspondence and better arrangement with wanted results. Whether in the domains of showcasing, exchange, administration, or individual connections, the marriage of workmanship and science in persuasion offers an integral asset for accomplishing one's goals.

CHAPTER 2

Building Trust And Credibility

Trust and credibility structure the bedrock whereupon viable persuasion is assembled. Whether in private connections, proficient undertakings, or any collaboration where you try to impact others, it is vital to lay out trust and credibility. In this complete conversation, we will investigate the meaning of trust and credibility as the underpinning of persuasion and dig into methodologies for their development.

The Significance of Trust and Credibility:

1. Trust as a Cornerstone: Trust is the key part of any fruitful relationship. It's the conviction that one can depend on the words, activities, and choices of another. Without trust, the underpinning of communication and impact becomes delicate.

2. Credibility as Currency: Credibility is the proportion of your capability, integrity, and skill. It permits people to have confidence in your insight and judgment. Credibility is the currency that supports trust.

3. Enhanced Communication: When trust and credibility are available, communication streams all the more easily. People are more open to tuning in, drawing in, and taking into account your point of view.

4. Risk Mitigation: In direction, trust and credibility diminish apparent gamble. At the point when people trust you, they are more able to take

risks or acknowledge your proposals since they accept you have their wellbeing on a fundamental level.

Strategies for Establishing Trust

1.   Consistency: Consistency in words and activities is the bedrock of trust. At the point when you consistently finish your responsibilities and adjust your activities to your words, you lay out a history of dependability.

2.   Transparency: Transparent communication cultivates trust. Be frank about your expectations, capacities, and impediments. Concede botches when they happen, as this can upgrade credibility.

3.   Competence: Showing skill and capability in your field is fundamental for credibility. Ceaselessly

foster your abilities and information, and be ready to share your mastery when it adds esteem.

4.   Empathy and Understanding: Show compassion by listening effectively and trying to grasp others' points of view and needs.
At the point when people feel appreciated and esteemed, it assembles trust.

5.   Integrity: Maintain high moral guidelines and moral standards. Your integrity is a key part of your credibility. Try not to think twice about values for transient additions.

6.   Reliability: Be consistent in fulfilling your responsibilities and time constraints. Unwavering quality is a foundation of trust. It incorporates being reliable, keeping commitments, and finishing liabilities.

7.   Effective Communication: Obviously and consciously articulate your considerations and

thoughts. Tailor your message to your crowd's necessities and inclinations. Great communication upgrades your credibility and trustworthiness.

8.   Testimonials and Social Proof: Use social verification and tributes from fulfilled clients, partners, or pertinent specialists. At the point when others vouch for your abilities, it supports your credibility.

9.   Long-Term Relationship Building: Develop long haul connections as opposed to zeroing in exclusively on quick gains. Consistent, long haul endeavors to assemble trust and credibility will yield enduring, valuable connections.

10.   Reputation Management: Gatekeeper your reputation and online presence. In the advanced age, your web-based reputation can fundamentally affect your trustworthiness and credibility.

In synopsis, trust and credibility are the foundations of viable persuasion. They support fruitful communication and the capacity to emphatically impact others. Utilizing systems like consistency, straightforwardness, ability, sympathy, and integrity can help you assemble and keep up with these significant parts. Thus, you upgrade your ability to convince as well as develop significant, enduring connections in view of shared trust and regard.

CHAPTER 3
Be Welcomed

The expression "do this and you will be welcomed anyplace" frequently implies the force of specific ways of behaving or characteristics that generally make a positive impression and cultivate acknowledgment. While it's fundamental to be authentic and adjust your way to deal with various circumstances, there are a few generally valued activities and properties that can make you more invite in different settings:

1. Respect: Recognize people's perspectives, time, and limits. Be respectful and chivalrous in your connections.

2. Active Listening: Give close consideration when others talk.

Show certifiable interest in what they need to say and ask follow-up inquiries to exhibit your commitment.

3. Empathy: Attempt to figure out the emotions and viewpoints of others. Show compassion by recognizing their sentiments and encounters.

4. Helpfulness: Offer help when proper. Helping other people, whether through thoughtful gestures or offering arrangements, can make you a welcome presence.

5. Honesty: Be honest and straightforward in your dealings. Genuineness constructs trust and credibility, making you a solid and trusted person.

6. Positive Attitude: Keep a positive and hopeful viewpoint. Energy is infectious and frequently draws people toward the individuals who transmit it.

7. Adaptability: Be available to alternate points of view and versatile to evolving circumstances. Adaptability and a readiness to team up are characteristics that make you a significant colleague.

8. Confidence: Task trust in your capacities and choices, as it can move trust in others too.

9. Appreciation: Show appreciation and appreciation when others help or back you. Recognizing their commitments reinforces connections.

10. Integrity: Maintain areas of strength for a moral code. People respect the individuals who make the wisest decision, in any event, while it's difficult.

11. Communication Skills: Foster viable communication abilities. Put yourself out there obviously and compactly, and be a decent audience.

Viable communication is a vital aspect for being invited in different settings.

12. Open-Mindedness: Be available to novel thoughts, societies, and encounters. A receptive demeanor can make you more congenial and comprehensive.

Being welcomed anywhere isn't tied in with being a chameleon or forfeiting your legitimacy. All things being equal, about epitomizing characteristics and ways of behaving advance positive communications and associations. Building connections, extending regard, and being a strong presence are key elements in causing others to see the value in your organization.

First Impression" They Say"

The idiom "first impression lasts longer" holds a lot of truth. First impressions are the underlying decisions and assessments people make about you when they first meet or experience you. These early appraisals can altogether impact how others see and associate with you. Here are a few motivations behind why first impressions matter:

1.   Lasting Impact: First effects will generally have an enduring effect. Once framed, they can be trying to change. People frequently anchor their perspectives on you in light of that underlying experience.

2.   Quick Choice Making: People make quick decisions as an endurance system. These on the spot judgment calls assist people with surveying possible dangers or partners. First impressions are essential for this intuitive dynamic interaction.

3. Confirmation Bias: Once a first impression is laid out, people will quite often look for proof that affirms their underlying judgment. This mental predisposition, known as the tendency to look for predetermined feedback, can build up the force of the first impression.

4. Relationship Building: In friendly and expert settings, framing positive first impressions is basic for building connections. A good underlying feeling can make you ready for future communications and participation.

5. Professional Success: In an expert setting, first impressions can influence your vocation. New employee screenings, gatherings with clients, and communications with partners all start with an appraisal of your expert picture.

6. Personal Attraction: In private connections, including dating and fellowships, the underlying

feeling can decide if somebody is keen on getting to realize you better.

7.   Credibility and Trust: Credibility and trust are many times in light of first impressions. On the off chance that you seem trustworthy and dependable in your underlying experience, people are bound to have faith as would be natural for you and activities.

To establish a positive first connection, consider factors like your appearance, non-verbal communication, demeanor, and communication abilities. Move toward experiences with an open and amiable disposition, listen effectively, and extend regard and thought for the other individual. While first impressions are critical, it's additionally essential to recall that people can change their viewpoints with time and rehashed corporations. In this way, consistently exhibiting your personality and skill is similarly fundamental for keeping a positive and enduring impression.

Communicating With People Easily

Speaking with people effectively includes the capacity to convey your contemplations, sentiments, and thoughts in a reasonable and viable way while cultivating positive associations. Key components for effective communication incorporate undivided attention, compassion, and adjusting your communication style to suit your crowd. Non-verbal signals, like non-verbal communication and manner of speaking, assume a vital part. Building affinity and trust, being brief and coordinated in your communication, and settling clashes usefully are likewise essential. The way to simple communication is a blend of abilities and mentalities that work with smooth and significant cooperations with others.

How To Attract People

Attracting people and cultivating connections is a diverse workmanship, enveloping a mix of characteristics, ways of behaving, and systems intended to make you connect with and engage. Here is an extensive comprehension of how to draw in people:

1.   Confidence: Certainty is attractive. It includes keeping up with self-assuredness, showing conviction, and extending confidence in your capacities. Certainty draws people toward you, as it reflects confidence and a conviction that all is good.

2.   Positive Attitude: Developing and keeping a positive and hopeful viewpoint is an irresistible quality. Energy is engaging, as it spreads and makes an inspiring climate that people normally incline toward.

3.   Active Listening: One of the principal parts of drawing in people is undivided attention.

It includes truly zeroing in on what others are talking about, clarifying pressing issues, and approving their sentiments. Undivided attention encourages significant connections.

4.   Empathy: Sympathy is the capacity to comprehend and recognize others' sentiments and viewpoints. Showing sympathy by truly thinking often about somebody's prosperity is significantly alluring.

5.   Sense of Humor: An advanced funny bone and the capacity to make people giggle are enormously engaging. Chuckling interfaces people, encourages bonds, and makes you more alluring.

6.   Interest in Others: Showing a genuine interest in others by getting some information about their lives, interests, and encounters is a vital part of fascination. At the point when people see that you really need to know them, it attracts them to you.

7.   Respect: Regard for others is a crucial structure block of fascination. Approaching others with deference and kindness makes a positive impression and attracts people nearer to you.

8.   Authenticity: Being legitimate and real is alluring. Legitimacy conveys genuineness and truthfulness, which people normally see as engaging. Professing to be somebody you're not will in general be a mood killer.

9.   Common Interests: Imparted interests and leisure activities to others give a characteristic connection point. Participating in exercises that line up with the interests of others makes you more engaging as a sidekick.

10. Confidence in Your Passions: Communicating trust in your interests and interests is infectious. At the point when you're energetic about something, that energy can make you more appealing to the individuals who share your inclinations.

11. Generosity: Offering and helping other people without expecting anything as a trade off is profoundly alluring. Liberality exhibits your kindness and thought.

12.   Physical Appearance: Dealing with your actual appearance, dressing great, and keeping up with great individual cleanliness can improve your allure.

13.   Active Lifestyle: A functioning and solid way of life passes imperativeness and responsibility on to prosperity, which is alluring to other people.

14.   Professional Competence: In an expert setting, being gifted, proficient, and skillful in your field is alluring to likely bosses, clients, or partners.

15.   Confidence in Your Abilities: Putting stock in your capacities and capabilities is alluring. Trust in your abilities can make you really engage in different settings.

16.   Open-Mindedness: Being available to new encounters, thoughts, and societies is alluring, making you fascinating and interesting to a different scope of people.

17.   Self-Improvement: A pledge to personal development through learning, self-improvement, or expertise advancement is viewed as alluring.

Making People Like You Instantly

Making a moment affability factor depends on the force of first impressions. Here is an extensive viewpoint on making people like you in a split second:

1. Smile: A certified and comforting grin is generally welcoming. At the point when you meet somebody with a well disposed grin, you quickly make a positive impression.

2. Eye Contact: Keeping in touch during discussions conveys mindfulness and interest. It makes you more amiable on the grounds that it extends regard and commitment.

3. Remembering Names: Recalling and utilizing somebody's name during a discussion mirrors that you value and regard them. This straightforward motion can quickly make a great impression.

4. Active Listening: Effectively standing by listening to what others say shows that you are truly

intrigued. Seek clarification on some pressing issues, offer smart reactions, and approve their sentiments. People like being heard.

5. Body Language: Open and positive non-verbal communication, like uncrossed arms, gesturing, and confronting the individual you're addressing, conveys agreeability and makes you all the more in a flash amiable.

6. Compliments: Offering true commendations when proper can make a great moment impression. Praises on accomplishments or appearance make you more affable.

7. Finding Normal Ground: Discover normal interests or encounters to associate over. Shared side interests or encounters can make a prompt bond.

8. Support and Encouragement: Show backing and consolation when somebody shares their objectives or dreams. Offering inspirational statements can in a flash make people like you.

9. Respecting Individual Boundaries: Regarding individual limits and staying away from intrusive or

awkward subjects during starting collaborations is a vital component of moment affability.

10. Expressing Enthusiasm: Show excitement while examining shared interests or normal themes. Your excitement can be irresistible and make you more affable.

11. Positivity: Keep an inspirational perspective and stay away from negative discussions or grumbling during introductory connections. Inspiration is appealing.

12. Flexibility: Be versatile and liberal. Being willing to investigate alternate points of view and thoughts can in a flash make you more agreeable.

13. Gratitude: Offering thanks when somebody helps or supports you makes altruism and amiability.

14. Kindness: Thoughtful gestures, whether little signals or accommodating activities, immediately make you more affable.

15. Authenticity: Being credible and consistent with yourself is a principal component of moment

agreeability. Credibility makes a certified impression.

By embracing these methodologies and being sensitive to the signs and needs of the people you meet, you can make a positive and quick effect, improving your agreeability and connection with others. While first impressions are huge, recall that they are the establishment for building further and additional getting through connections.

How To Make People Reason With You

Making people reason with you includes successful correspondence and persuasion. To accomplish this, think about these methodologies:

1. Active Listening: Start by listening effectively to the next individual. Show that you esteem their viewpoint and are available to their thoughts. This creates an establishment for a useful discourse.

2.	Empathize:	Attempt to understand their perspective and sentiments. Identifying with their interests and emotions can make them more responsive to your viewpoints.

3.	Respect Their Perspective:	Regardless of whether you dissent, regard their entitlement to hold their viewpoint. Try not to excuse their thoughts by and large, as this can prompt protectiveness.

4.	Clear Communication:	Offer your viewpoints obviously and compactly. Stay away from language or overly complex language. Be immediate, so your focuses are handily perceived.

5.	Back Your Claims:	Use proof, realities, and legitimate reasoning to help your arguments. Giving information or models can make your position seriously convincing.

6.   Build Trust: Trust is fundamental for persuasion. Lay out trust by being solid, steady, and genuine in your connections.

7.   Find Common Ground: Recognize shared values or objectives. Featuring common ground can create a feeling of unity and make it more straightforward for others to reason with you.

8.   Ask Unassuming Questions: Urge them to think by posing unconditional inquiries that quick reflection. This can invigorate a more profound understanding of the subject.

9.   Avoid Arguments: Avoid conflicts or arguments. All things being equal, center around a cooperative and deferential conversation.

10.   Patience: Give them an opportunity to assimilate and handle the data. People might require time to adjust their perspectives or think about alternative viewpoints.

11.   Appeal to Emotions: While depending on realities and rationale is significant, don't underrate the force of emotions. Use stories or models that reverberate with their emotions to put forth your defense more powerful.

12.   Use the "Because" Technique: While making a solicitation or argument, give a reason utilizing "because." Studies have shown that just contributing a reason, regardless of whether it's fairly self-evident, can increment consistency.

13.   Offer Alternatives: Give practical alternatives or compromises that address their interests while lining up with your objectives.

14.   Be Open to Compromise: Exhibiting a readiness to find center ground shows your reasonableness and urges others to do likewise.

15.   Respect Non-Verbal Cues: Focus on non-verbal prompts, like non-verbal communication and manner of speaking. Change your methodology in the event that you sense opposition or uneasiness.

16.   Appeal to Shared Values: Casing your arguments concerning values or rules that you both hold dear. This can be a strong method for presenting your defense more influential.

17.   Stay Quiet and Polite: Hold your emotions in line and keep a conscious tone. Emotional eruptions or impoliteness can ruin reasoning and close off useful discussion.

18.   Follow Up: After the conversation, circle back to them. This shows your continuous commitment to the discussion and can prompt further reasoning.

Not everyone will constantly concur with you, however by utilizing these techniques, you can improve the probability that people will be more able to reason with you and participate in helpful discourse.

You Can't Eat your Cake And Have It

"You can't eat your cake and have it" is a well known saying that features the idea of compromises and decisions. With regards to winning arguments, it recommends that few out of every odd argument can be won or that endeavoring to "have it all" in an argument is frequently unreasonable.

The following are a couple of central issues to consider:

1. Not All Arguments Are Winnable: In numerous conversations and discussions, there might be no outright "winner." People frequently have alternate points of view, encounters, and values, making it trying to totally persuade others.

2.   Respect Varying Views: Perceiving that you can't win every argument supports the significance of contrasting viewpoints. It's beneficial to take part in conversations and gain from each other, regardless of whether you convince somebody to change their position.

3.   Choose Your Battles: It's fundamental to pick your fights and conclude which arguments merit your significant investment. Now and then, it's more useful to relinquish minor conflicts and spotlight on additional significant issues.

4.   Maintain Relationships: Overly forceful or angry conduct in arguments can harm connections. Understanding that you can't necessarily in all cases win every argument supports a more compassionate and circumspect methodology.

5.   Seek Common Ground: As opposed to attempting to "win" an argument, plan to figure out

something worth agreeing on and fabricate scaffolds of understanding. This can prompt more valuable and less antagonistic collaborations.

In rundown, the colloquialism "you can't eat your cake and have it" fills in as an update that not all arguments can be won through and through, and once in a while, the pursuit of understanding and shared regard is more significant than winning a discussion. It energizes a reasonable and insightful way to deal with conflicts and conversations.

How To Avoid Making Enemies

Winning people over and trying not to create foes can be accomplished through a strategic and thoughtful methodology. Here are a few systems to assist you with accomplishing this sensitive equilibrium:

1.   Listen Actively: Give close consideration to other people and exhibit that you esteem their viewpoints and sentiments. Undivided attention cultivates regard and understanding.

2.   Respect Differences: Recognize that people have various viewpoints and backgrounds. Regard these distinctions and try not to excuse or criticize them.

3.   Empathize: Come at the situation from others' perspective to understand their viewpoints and emotions. Showing empathy can go far in building affinity and keeping away from struggle.

4.   Stay Quiet and Respectful: Keep a quiet and conscious disposition, in any event, while examining combative issues. Keep away from angry or forceful ways of behaving that can prompt animosity.

5.   Find Common Ground: Distinguish shared interests, values, or objectives as an establishment for your connections. Zeroing in on commonalities can create a feeling of unity.

6.   Offer Alternatives: As opposed to forcing your viewpoint, give alternatives or compromises that address worries while lining up with your objectives.

7. Pick Fights Admirably: Only one out of every odd conflict merits going after. Be particular in the arguments you participate in and prioritize issues that genuinely matter.

8.   Avoid Blame: When conflicts emerge, try not to fault or point fingers. Center around finding arrangements as opposed to harping on previous oversights.

9.   Stay Open-Minded: Be available to the possibility of adjusting your perspective or adjusting your position in light of new data or alternate points of view.

10. Respect Boundaries: Regard individual limits and try not to push somebody past their usual range of familiarity. Perceive when it's suitable to step back and let an issue rest.

11.   Use "I" Statements: Edge your assertions utilizing "I" as opposed to "you." For instance, say, "I feel" or "I think," to offer your viewpoints without sounding accusatory.

12.   Conflict Goal Skills: Learn and rehearse powerful compromise abilities, for example, finding win arrangements and splitting the difference.

13.   Apologize When Necessary: On the off chance that you commit an error or unintentionally irritate somebody,

offer a genuine statement of regret. Saying 'sorry' shows humility and a readiness to set things right.

14.   Build Trust: Lay out trust through consistency, reliability, and straightforwardness in your communications. Trust is fundamental for positive connections.

15.   Follow Up: After conversations or conflicts, circle back to people to beware of their prosperity and show your commitment to keeping a positive relationship.

16.   Accept Differences: Some of the time, it's fundamental to acknowledge that not everyone will be prevailed upon or that a few conflicts are hopeless. In such cases, it's ideal to part agreeably as opposed to driving an issue.

Winning people over isn't tied in with causing them to submit to your views yet about building significant associations and cultivating understanding. Make progress toward positive associations that leave space for contrasts while zeroing in on shared objectives and values.

Admit, If You Are Wrong

Admitting When You Are Wrong: An Indication of Solidarity and Integrity

Admitting one's slip-ups is a central part of self-awareness, keeping up with sound connections, and showing integrity. This understanding investigates the most common way of admitting when you are wrong and the significance it holds in different parts of life.

Perceiving the Mistake:
The excursion of admitting one's mix-up starts with mindfulness. At the point when you understand that you have made a blunder, it is essential to stop and think about the situation. Recognizing the slip-up, regardless of how little or significant, is the most

important phase simultaneously. This self-recognition establishes the groundwork for tending to the blunder.

Taking Responsibility:

When you perceive the mix-up, it is fundamental to take on an obligation. Stay away from the impulse to shift fault onto others or rationalize. Assuming liability exhibits accountability and a commitment to ethical ways of behaving. By saying, "I made a blunder," you obviously convey responsibility for both.

Fair Admission:

Utilize clear and succinct language to admit your misstep. Trustworthiness and straightforwardness in admitting the blunder are fundamental. Stay away from any type of trickery, as it can disintegrate trust and credibility. A legit confirmation is a demonstration of your integrity and character.

Saying 'sorry' and Repairing:

If your misstep has impacted or burdened others, offering an earnest statement of regret is an act of kindness. An expression of remorse shows that you understand the effect of your blunder on others and empathize with their situation. It can assist with retouching stressed connections and advance pardoning.

Giving a Solution:

Where conceivable, give the right data or an answer to rectify your slip-up. Making a move to address the mistake shows your commitment to exactness and critical thinking. It additionally mirrors your devotion to making things right.

Learning and Improvement:

Admitting your slip-up isn't the finish of the interaction; it's the start of development. In the wake of admitting the mistake, find an opportunity to think about why it happened and how to forestall it later on. Gaining from your missteps is an important part of individual and expert turn of events.

Empowering Feedback:

To acquire a superior understanding of what your slip-up meant for others and how to forestall comparative mistakes, energize input. Useful criticism can give bits of knowledge and assist you with turning out to be more mindful of your activities and their results.

Keeping up with Professionalism:

No matter what, it is fundamental to keep up with impressive skill while admitting an error. Try not to become cautious or angry. Effortlessly admitting your mistake upgrades your credibility and encourages a climate of regard.

Modifying Trust:

If trust has been impacted because of your misstep, do whatever it takes to revamp it.

Reliably exhibiting reliability and precision over time can assist with recapturing trust and strengthen connections.

Remaining Open to Input:

Proceeding to remain open to include and useful criticism from others is a proactive way to deal with blunder counteraction. By seeking and embracing input, you can upgrade your mindfulness and try not to repeat comparative errors.

In synopsis, admitting when you are wrong is definitely not an indication of shortcoming; it is an indication of solidarity and integrity. It mirrors a commitment to genuineness, accountability, and persistent personal development. By embracing this training, you can encourage better connections, gain regard, and add to your own and proficient turn of events.

CHAPTER 4

The Wonder-Working Formula

Persuasion is a complicated workmanship, and the wonder-working formula of persuasion incorporates an assortment of methodologies and principles that can significantly upgrade your ability to really impact others. This cognizance gives an inside and out investigation of this formula, featuring the key components that add to effective persuasion.

Understanding the Principles:

1. Ethos, Pathos, and Logos:

The wonder-working formula of persuasion draws from Aristotle's old style methods of persuasion: ethos (ethical appeal), pathos (emotional appeal), and logos (legitimate appeal).

Ethos includes laying out credibility and trust, pathos takes advantage of the crowd's emotions, and logos depend on realities and rationale. A balanced powerful argument incorporates every one of the three to draw in both the level headed and emotional sides of the crowd.

1.   Ethical Foundation: Persuasion starts with an ethical foundation. Ethical persuasion is based on principles of trustworthiness, straightforwardness, and regard for the independence and upsides of others. It guarantees that the persuasion interaction depends on sound moral and ethical grounds.

2.   Empathy and Understanding: The wonder-working formula of persuasion prioritizes empathy and understanding. To convince successfully, you should appreciate the viewpoints, necessities, and emotions of your crowd. Relating to their interests lays out a vital association.

3.   Active Listening: Undivided attention is a foundation of convincing correspondence. By effectively captivating with your crowd, seeking clarification on pressing issues, and exhibiting veritable interest, you create a climate of common regard and significant exchange.

4.   Credibility and Trust: Laying out your credibility is fundamental. People are bound to be convinced by those they trust and view as specialists. Building trust is a continuous interaction that depends on consistency, reliability, and straightforwardness.

5. Making a Convincing Message:

An enticing message should be convincing and locking in. It ought to get the notice of your crowd, obviously present your argument or proposition, and be organized intelligently. Viable persuasion frequently includes appealing to both the normal and emotional parts of your crowd's dynamic interaction.

Building the Framework:

6. Clear Communication: Persuasion necessitates clear and brief correspondence. Express your arguments, thoughts, and recommendations in a clear way. Keep away from language or tangled language to guarantee that your message is effectively perceived.

7. Framing and Storytelling: Viable persuasion frequently includes outlining your message in a convincing and engaging story. Storytelling draws in emotions and creates an association between your crowd and the message you seek to pass on.

9. Overcoming Objections:

The wonder-working formula of persuasion perceives that protests and obstruction are common. Tending to complaints straightforwardly, consciously, and influentially exhibits your capability and can overcome hindrances to understanding.

10.   Appeal to Emotions: Persuasion envelops a harmony among rationale and emotions. Emotional appeal can be a useful asset in impacting choices. Summoning the right emotions can solidify your argument and make it significant.

Executing Strategies:

11.   Social Proof: Influence the guideline of social confirmation, which proposes that people are bound to follow a strategy if they see others doing likewise. Featuring tributes, supports, or instances of comparative achievement can be powerful.

12.   Reciprocity: Reciprocity proposes that people are learned to answer well when given something. Offering worth or help without expecting quick returns can set off a feeling of responsibility, improving the probability of consistency.

13. Scarcity: The scarcity guideline features that items or opportunities seen as scant are more appealing. Applying this rule, you can create a need to get moving and exclusivity, empowering your crowd to make a move.

14. Consistency and Commitment: Empowering consistency and commitment can prompt greater consistency. By inciting little initial commitments or lining up with existing convictions, you can fabricate a foundation for additional significant arrangements.

Adjusting and Evaluating:

15. Feedback and Adaptation: Effective persuasion includes adaptability. Seeking and coordinating criticism permits you to change your methodology, tweak your message, and take special care of the advancing requirements and inclinations of your crowd.

16.   Evaluation and Consistent Improvement: A wonder-working formula of persuasion doesn't depend on a decent arrangement of strategies yet underscores persistent improvement. Assessing the results of your persuasion endeavors and gaining from the two victories and disappointments is critical.

The wonder-working formula of persuasion is a multifaceted methodology that joins ethical principles, powerful correspondence, and key execution. It depends on empathy, credibility, and adaptability to effectively connect with and impact others. By understanding and applying these components, you can improve your powerful abilities and accomplish your ideal results in different individual and expert settings.

What Everybody Wants

With regards to persuasion, understanding what people need or want can be a significant instrument for impacting their choices and activities. While individual longings and inspirations can fluctuate, a few common cravings frequently become an integral factor while convincing others:

1. Trust and Credibility: People need to accept and confide in the individual or source conveying a powerful message. Showing dependability and credibility is fundamental to acquiring their certainty.

2. Relevance: Crowds need to see the pertinence of the message to their own lives and interests. Persuasion is more powerful when the message lines up with what is important to them.

3. Benefits and Value: People by and large seek to acquire something from their activities.

Powerful messages ought to underscore the benefits and worth of the proposed activity or thought.

4.   Emotional Connection: People are driven by emotions. Persuasion frequently depends on creating an emotional association with the crowd, whether through positive sentiments .

5.   Security and Safety: Numerous individuals want security and wellbeing. If your message can pass on that the proposed activity upgrades security or lessens chances, it can be more influential.

6.   Belonging and Social Acceptance: People need to have a place and feel acknowledged by their gatherings. Persuasion can take advantage of this craving by showing how the proposed activity lines up with the qualities and standards of their community.

7.   Fulfillment of Needs: Enticing messages that address essential human necessities, like food, safe

house, love, and confidence, are frequently compelling. Understand and appeal to these requirements in your persuasion endeavors.

8.   Positive Outcomes: People for the most part need positive results from their choices. Your influential message ought to stress the potential for progress and positive outcomes.

9.   Solutions to Problems: Individuals need answers for their concerns or difficulties. Persuasion can be exceptionally powerful when it offers pragmatic arrangements and addresses pain points.

10.   Ease and Convenience: Many people seek simplicity and comfort in their lives. Persuasion can zero in on how the proposed activity is straightforward, available, or efficient.

11.   Freedom and Autonomy: While people might want direction, they likewise need to feel in charge

and independent. Persuasion ought to regard this craving for personal organization.

12. Clarity and Understanding: Enticing messages ought to be clear and straightforward. People need to get a handle on the message's substance and intent rapidly and without any problem.

13. Validation and Recognition: Recognition and approval of one's opinions and decisions are strong inspirations. Acknowledging and validating your crowd's viewpoints can improve the convincingness of your message.

14. Personal Development and Improvement: Appeals to personal development and personal growth can be exceptionally convincing. Demonstrate the way that the proposed activity or thought can assist individuals with becoming better variants of themselves.

15. Emotional and Mental Satisfaction: People frequently seek emotional and mental fulfillment. Persuasion can take advantage of these cravings by addressing emotional necessities like happiness, certainty, and true serenity.

Understanding these common cravings and incorporating them into your powerful messages can increase the probability of effectively influencing others. Tailoring your way to deal with what people need can put forth your persuasion attempts more powerful and compelling.

An Appeal We Are All Attracted To

With regards to persuasion, there are certain appeals that will generally all around draw in people and improve the adequacy of your convincing endeavors. One such appeal is the "WIIFM" factor :

WIIFM (How might this benefit Me): This appeal takes advantage of the inherent personal circumstance of individuals. While crafting powerful messages, highlighting the benefits and benefits for the crowd, and demonstrating how your proposition or thought lines up with their personal interests and needs, is a generally appealing methodology.

Here's the reason the "WIIFM" factor is so compelling in persuasion:

1.   Relevance: It makes the message straightforwardly pertinent to the individual, showing them that you understand their interests and targets.

2. Personal Benefit: People are normally attracted to opportunities that offer personal benefits, whether it's saving time, cash, exertion, or improving their prosperity.

3. Motivation: When you show how your proposition lines up with the crowd's objectives and wants, it spurs them to make a move.

4. Clarity: It gives an unmistakable and direct reason for why the crowd ought to consider your proposition or thought, making it simple for them to understand.

5. Empathy: Demonstrating that you've thought about their necessities and are addressing them can create an emotional association and empathy, making your message really appealing.

6. Alignment with Self-Interest: People are normally self-interested, and they frequently pursue choices in view of how those choices will benefit them.

7. Solving Problems: By showing how your proposition takes care of an issue or satisfies a

requirement for the crowd, you appeal to their longing for arrangements and improvement.

8. Motivating Action: The "WIIFM" appeal can be a strong inspiration for activity, encouraging the crowd to make the strides you're advocating.

By aligning your powerful message with the "WIIFM" factor, you can make your proposition all the more appealing and increase its effect. It's a clear and compelling method for connecting with people's inherent personal responsibility and guiding them toward the ideal choice or activity.

Try This, When Nothing Else Works

1. FEEL-FELT-FOUND"

At the point when other persuasion procedures have fizzled, and you're faced with an especially challenging situation, you can consider the "feel-felt-found" approach. It involves empathizing with the individual you're trying to convince by acknowledging their feelings, sharing that others have felt the same way, and explaining what those individuals eventually found or discovered. This is the secret:

1. Empathize (Feel):   Start by acknowledging and validating the other individual's feelings or concerns. Tell them that you understand the reason why they feel the manner in which they do. This shows that you regard their viewpoint and are empathetic to their emotions.

2.   Relate (Felt):   Offer a story or illustration of somebody, including yourself or others, who has felt in basically the same manner previously. This assists the individual with realizing that they are in good company in their feelings and concerns. It creates a feeling of relatability.

3.　　Reveal (Found):　　Presently, share what those individuals (including yourself or others) eventually found or discovered in the wake of working through the situation or concern. Feature how their initial reservations were settled or the way in which their activities prompted positive results. This gives an answer or a way ahead.

For instance, if you're trying to convince somebody to assume another liability at work, you could say: "I understand how taking on this new responsibility could appear to be overwhelming. Others in the group have felt the same way when they were first asked. Notwithstanding, what they found is that it gave them new opportunities for development, and it really worked on their abilities and profession possibilities."

The "feel-felt-found" approach is a method for empathizing, relating, and offering an answer, which can be compelling when other persuasion strategies haven't worked. It shows that you understand the individual's interests, others have been in a comparative situation, and there is a positive way ahead.

2. DOOR-IN-THE-FACE

At the point when traditional convincing methodologies aren't working, it can be useful to utilize a procedure known as the "door-in-the-face" technique. This approach involves presenting an initial, seemingly unreasonable solicitation that is probably going to be denied (the "big ask"). After the big ask is dismissed, you circle back to a more safe solicitation that you really intended to propose all along (the "little ask"). This is the carefully guarded secret:

1. Start with the Big Ask: Begin your persuasion endeavor by making a solicitation that you expect will be declined. This initial solicitation ought to be significant and more demanding than what you really care about. The objective is to create a feeling

of difference between the big task and your definitive objective.

2.   Prepare for Rejection: Guess that the big ask will be declined. Be prepared for the dismissal, and don't get deterred by it.

3.   Follow Up with the Little Ask: After the big ask is dismissed, quickly present your valid and more reasonable solicitation (the little ask). This more modest solicitation is what you intended to propose all along.

4.   Highlight the Concession: When you present the little ask, notice that you understand the big ask was quite challenging and that you value the other party's willingness to think twice about it. Underline the concession you are making by offering the more modest solicitation.

5.   Explain the Reasoning: Give reasons to why the little ask is a fair and worthwhile proposition.

Explain how it benefits the two players and addresses the worries that prompted the initial dismissal of the big task.

This door-in-the-face strategy uses the mental principle of reciprocity and the differentiation impact. People frequently feel inclined to respond after a concession has been made, making them bound to consent to the more modest, more reasonable solicitation. Additionally, the difference between the big and little tasks can cause the little to ask to show up better in examinations.

While this technique can be effective, it should be used judiciously and ethically. It's important to ensure that both the big and small tasks are reasonable and that the approach aligns with your ethical standards. Overusing this technique or making unreasonable big asks can backfire and harm your credibility.

3. SOCRATIC QUESTIONING

At the point when traditional powerful techniques don't appear to be compelling, it's a chance to utilize a different methodology. Here is a methodology to attempt when nothing else works:

Instead of straightforwardly presenting your arguments or recommendations, utilize Socratic questioning. This strategy involves asking inquiries without a right or wrong answer that guide the individual toward your ideal decision. By leading them to consider the points you need to make through a progression of very much created questions, you permit them to show up at the choice themselves. This can be more influential because it connects with their critical thinking and energizes responsibility for thought.

Socratic questioning could appear as though this: "Might you at any point assist me with understanding the reason why this approach has been fruitful for others previously? What benefits do you see in considering this arrangement?"

By using Socratic questioning, you urge the individual to effectively partake in the dynamic cycle and may find that they are more open to your viewpoint when they feel they've arrived at the resolution all alone.

CHAPTER 5
Staying Resilient

In the excursion of persuasion and influence, difficulties, dismissals, and failures are inevitable. Nonetheless, what separates fruitful persuaders is their versatility in the face of adversity. Section 9 spotlights on the craft of staying tough and embracing difficulties as opportunities for development. It dives into how to handle difficulties and dismissals, maintain motivation and concentration, and concentrate on important illustrations from failure.

Handling Setbacks and Rejections

- The Idea of Setbacks: This part investigates the different types of misfortunes and dismissals that one could experience in the persuasion cycle. It underlines that these difficulties are not failures but rather opportunities for development.

- Flexibility Strategies: Reasonable systems for developing versatility are talked about. These include reframing mishaps as learning encounters, maintaining a development mindset, and seeking criticism to work on future endeavors.

- Overcoming Mental Barriers: Dealing with the emotional effect of dismissal and overcoming self-question is tended to. Strategies for managing gloomy emotions are introduced to maintain certainty.

Staying Motivated and Focused

This part features the significance of motivation in the persuasion cycle. It examines the significance of setting clear objectives and maintaining energy for your targets.

1. Define Your "Why": To remain roused, have an unmistakable understanding of why you need to win people over. This feeling of direction can fuel your endeavors in any event, when faced with difficulties.

2. Set Clear Goals: Lay out specific, feasible objectives that give guidance and a feeling of achievement. These achievements can assist with maintaining your motivation.

3. Visualize Success: Create a psychological picture of your enticing achievement.

Representation can be a strong inspiration by making your objectives feel more attainable.

4. Stay Organized: Compelling using time productively and association are significant for maintaining the center. Prioritize tasks and allot your energy astutely.

5. Celebrate Little Wins: Recognize and commend your accomplishments, regardless of how little. This positive reinforcement can support motivation.

6. Seek Support: Encircle yourself with an encouraging group of people of companions, tutors, or friends who can give consolation and direction.

Learning from Failure

- Failure as a Learning Opportunity: This segment reevaluates failure as an important learning opportunity. It urges individuals to view mishaps as input and opportunities for development rather than as indications of incompetence. Versatility begins with a mindset shift. Rather than viewing difficulties and dismissals as failures, consider them to be opportunities for development and learning.

- Extracting Lessons: Useful strategies for extracting examples from failure are introduced. These include conducting after death investigations, seeking outside viewpoints, and identifying specific regions for development.

- Implementing Improvements: The final piece of this segment explains how to try the examples learned. It tends to the significance of making substantial changes and continually evolving your enticing methodologies.

CHAPTER 6
Winning People Over In Different Contexts

Chapter 6 of our complete manual for persuasion digs into the multifaceted universe of powerful correspondence in different settings. Every part investigates how persuasion strategies can be successfully applied in distinct everyday issues, addressing special difficulties and opportunities.

Persuasion in the Workplace

In the cutting edge proficient landscape, persuasion is a foundation expertise. This part uncovers the methodologies and strategies fundamental for succeeding in the working environment:

- Influencing Associates and Superiors: Successfully persuading partners and bosses is vital for advancing your profession, garnering support for your thoughts, and promoting coordinated effort within groups.

- Navigating Office Politics: Work environment elements frequently involve intricate politics. Learning how to explore these politics while maintaining integrity and persuading really is an important expertise.

- Leading with Persuasion: Successful initiative frequently hinges on influential abilities. Whether you're leading a group or a whole association, knowing how to inspire and persuade others is critical.

- Negotiating for Profession Advancement: Powerful exchange assumes a vital part in securing pay raises, advancements, and other professional successes. This section gives insights into mastering this workmanship.

- Handling Working environment Conflicts: Struggle is inevitable in the work environment.

Persuasion can be a significant instrument for resolving debates and fostering an agreeable workplace.

Winning over Companions and Family

Persuasion in personal connections is a fragile dance of empathy and understanding. This section investigates the interpersonal abilities important for:

-       Resolving Clashes with Cherished Ones: Conflicts and misunderstandings are common in personal connections. Learning how to address these contentions powerfully is fundamental for maintaining solid securities.

-    Persuading Relatives on Significant Decisions: From significant life decisions to everyday issues, knowing how to win over relatives can prompt more agreeable connections.

-       Strengthening Friendships: Building and maintaining kinships requires successful correspondence and persuasion. This part offers insights into fostering profound and lasting associations.

- Using Persuasion to Cultivate Associations and Understanding: Whether it's with family or companions, understanding the principles of powerful correspondence can prompt more meaningful and empathetic connections.

Persuasion in Sales and Marketing

Sales and marketing are domains where the specialty of persuasion is fundamental. This part investigates the systems, methods, and brain research behind:

- Convincing Clients to Purchase Items or Services: Persuasion is at the core of sales. Understanding how to identify and address client issues while addressing complaints is vital to progress.

- Crafting Powerful Marketing Campaigns: Marketing involves capturing consideration and convincing buyers to make a move. Discover the brain research and techniques behind enticing marketing.

- Building Brand Loyalty: Persuasion assumes a critical part in fostering brand faithfulness. Investigate how to make clients purchase once as well as return again and again.

- Handling Protests and Dismissals in Sales: Dismissals are a piece of sales. Learning how to handle protests powerfully can turn a "no" into a "yes."

Public Speaking and Leadership

In positions of authority and public speaking, persuasion is fundamental for inspiring, influencing, and motivating others. This part offers insights into:

- Delivering Powerful Talks and Presentations: Public speaking requires the ability to influence a group of people. This part dives into methods for delivering effective talks and introductions.

- Inspiring and Leading Teams: Viable initiative involves persuading and motivating a group to accomplish common objectives. Figure out how to lead with persuasion and inspiration.

- Communicating Really in Administration Roles: Authority frequently demands powerful correspondence with various partners. Investigate how persuasion can assist pioneers with communicating their vision and objectives all the more really.

- Harnessing the Influential Ability in Public and Motivational Speaking: Public and motivational speakers use persuasion to associate with their crowd on an emotional level and drive positive change.

Whether it's the expert field, personal connections, sales and marketing, or administration and public speaking, understanding and mastering the craft of persuasion is instrumental in achieving your objectives and influencing others positively. Every part gives significant methodologies and important insights for adapting your convincing abilities to the specific difficulties of every unique situation.

CHAPTER 7
The Ethics Of Persuasion

Ethical contemplations are a critical part of persuasion. This part investigates the fragile harmony between ethical persuasion and manipulation, emphasizing the significance of maintaining integrity in every single enticing exertion.

The Morals of Persuasion:

- Regard for Autonomy: Ethical persuasion regards individuals' independence and their entitlement to pursue informed choices. It involves presenting information genuinely and allowing people to pursue decisions that line up with their qualities.

- Transparency: Ethical persuasion requires straightforwardness and trustworthiness. Information ought not be disguised or mutilated to accomplish wanted results.

- Beneficence: Ethical persuasion seeks to benefit the two players involved. It ought to advance prosperity, shared gain, and positive results.

- Non-Coercion: Persuasion ought to never cross into coercion. People ought not be compelled, threatened, or maneuvered toward making rulings against their will.

- Informed Consent: Ethical persuasion guarantees that individuals have all the information they need to pursue informed choices. They ought to understand the outcomes and alternatives prior to choosing.

The Fine Line Between Persuasion and Manipulation

Coercion vs. Influence: The key distinction lies in the utilization of coercion. While persuasion involves influencing others through reasoning and emotional appeal, manipulation utilizes strategies that limit an individual's ability to go with a free decision.

- Trickery vs. Honesty: Manipulation frequently depends on trickery, while ethical persuasion depends on genuineness and straightforwardness. Controllers might utilize misleading statements, lies, or bogus vows to accomplish their objectives.

- Regard vs. Exploitation: Ethical persuasion regards the independence and upsides of individuals, whereas manipulation seeks to exploit vulnerabilities or shortcomings.

- Long haul vs. Transient Goals: Ethical persuasion frequently considers long haul results and plans to fabricate trust and lasting connections. Manipulation is regularly silly and may harm connections all the while.

- Common Benefit vs. Self-Gain: Ethical persuasion seeks common benefit, whereas manipulation frequently prioritizes the controller's personal responsibility.

Maintaining Integrity

- Self-Reflection: To maintain integrity in persuasion, individuals should participate in self-reflection. Think about the morals of your activities and motivations.

- Regard for Others: Recognize the qualities, independence, and decisions of others. Stay away from strategies that belittle or hurt them.

- Balancing Interests: Endeavor to find common ground and harmony between your interests and the interests of those you are persuading.

- Continuous Learning: Stay informed about ethical principles and best practices in persuasion. Schooling and personal development are fundamental for maintaining integrity.

- Accountability: Be responsible for your activities. If you perceive that you have acted unethically, assume liability and offer to set things right.

- Seek Feedback: Urge criticism from others to check the ethicality of your influential endeavors. Legit input can help you course-right when required.

In outline, the ethics of persuasion rotate around regard, straightforwardness, and the advancement of common benefit. It's fundamental to be watchful about the fine line between ethical persuasion and manipulation. Maintaining integrity in all powerful endeavors isn't simply an ethical objective yet in addition a critical figure building trust, credibility, and long haul connections.

CHAPTER 8
The Art Of Negotiation And Compromise

Negotiation and compromise are crucial abilities in the craft of persuasion. This part investigates the intricacies of negotiation, from the foundational abilities to the systems for achieving win arrangements, all while emphasizing the force of give and take and the significance of finding center ground to agree.

Negotiation Skills:

-    Dynamic Listening: Compelling negotiation starts with undivided attention. Understanding the viewpoints, needs, and worries of the other party is vital for finding common ground.

- Communication: Clear and open correspondence is fundamental in negotiations. Articulate your points actually and ask clarifying inquiries to stay away from misunderstandings.

- Issue Solving: Negotiation frequently involves critical thinking. The ability to identify issues and produce arrangements is a key expertise.

- Empathy: Understanding the emotions and motivations of the other party can prompt more useful negotiations. Demonstrating empathy can cultivate altruism.

- Patience: Negotiations might take time. Persistence is vital for maintaining a helpful atmosphere and arriving at commonly OK arrangements.

Strategies for Successful Negotiation:

-       BATNA (Best Alternative to an Arranged Agreement):   Understanding your BATNA and the BATNA of the other party gives a significant framework to negotiation.

-       Anchoring: Anchoring involves setting the initial terms of negotiation for your potential benefit. Talented mediators can utilize this strategy decisively.

-       Concession Management: Knowing when and how to make concessions is pivotal. Successful administration of concessions can prompt improved results.

-       Building Trust: Trust is the foundation of successful negotiations. Building and maintaining trust is a drawn out system.

- Social Awareness: Social differences can significantly influence negotiations. Being mindful of social subtleties is fundamental for worldwide negotiations.

Win-Win Solutions:

- Collaboration: A win arrangement frequently requires joint effort rather than a lose situation. Finding ways of satisfying the interests of all gatherings is the objective.

- Interest-Put together Negotiation: Focusing with respect to the interests, rather than positions, of the gatherings can prompt more creative arrangements.

- Creative Issue Solving: Thinking fresh and exploring unusual arrangements can open new roads for win results.

- Long haul Relationships: Think about the effect of the negotiation on your drawn out relationship with the other party. Take a stab at agreements that improve, rather than strain, your relationship.

The Power of Compromise:

- Common Give and Take: Compromise involves shared concessions. It's the craft of finding a center ground that fulfills the center interests of the two players.

- Flexibility: Being available to think twice about flexibility and adaptability. It's an indication of willingness to find arrangements.

- Preserving Relationships: Compromise can save connections and keep debates from escalating.

- Exchange offs: Powerful trade off frequently requires compromises. Identify what you're willing to surrender in return for what you need.

Finding Common Ground:

- Identify Shared Interests: Discover the common interests that can shape the reason for a center ground.

- Prioritize Issues: Rank the main things by significance. This helps in focusing on the most critical issues when seeking to split the difference.

- Create Options: Brainstorm numerous answers to find a center ground that obliges the interests, everything being equal.

Achieving Agreement:

- Formalizing Agreements: Guarantee that agreements are formalized in an unmistakable and legitimately binding way.

- Follow-Up: After an agreement is reached, follow-up to guarantee that all gatherings are fulfilling their commitments.

- Continuous Communication: Maintain open correspondence to resolve any issues or debates that might emerge after the agreement.

In outline, the specialty of negotiation and compromise is a focal component of persuasion. The ability to haggle successfully, utilize key abilities, find win arrangements, tackle the force of give and take, and arrive at agreements that fulfill all gatherings is fundamental in both expert and personal settings.

CONCLUSION

The excursion of persuasion is a dynamic and lifelong journey that traverses across different parts of our personal and expert lives. As we finish up this comprehensive aide, it's clear that the specialty of winning people over is a diverse and intricate interaction. Here, we consider the critical focal points and the way to becoming an expert of persuasion.

All through this aide, we've investigated the following:

1.   The Basics of Persuasion: We started by understanding the brain research of persuasion and the science behind convincing others. By delving into the intricacies of human independent direction, we established areas of strength for a point for our excursion.

2.   Building Trust and Credibility: Trust and credibility are the foundations of persuasion. We examined systems for establishing trust, which is fundamental for any convincing exertion.

3.   Effective Communication: The craft of communicating with people effectively and really is a significant expertise. We figured out how to adjust our correspondence style to associate with others.

4.   Attracting People: Attracting and making people like you instantly is an important expertise in persuasion. We investigated strategies for building quick compatibility.

5.   Making People Reason with You: Persuasion frequently involves normal arguments. We uncovered systems for engaging in sensible, all around reasoned conversations.

6.   Admitting When You're Wrong: Admitting your missteps is an indication of humility and can

upgrade your influential power. We talked about the significance of acknowledging when you're wrong.

7.   The Wonder Working Formula of Persuasion: We revealed a comprehensive view of persuasion, emphasizing empathy, authenticity, and ethical practices as fundamental parts.

8.   Understanding What Everybody Wants: Knowing the widespread cravings that people share is vital for tailoring your convincing endeavors to actually associate with others.

9.   Ethical Considerations: The ethical elements of persuasion are urgent. We investigated the fine line between persuasion and manipulation and the basics of maintaining integrity.

10.   Negotiation and Compromise: The specialty of negotiation and compromise assumes a significant part in persuasion. We examined the

systems and abilities fundamental for achieving win arrangements and center ground agreements.

11.   The Journey's End: Our journey closes with the understanding that becoming a pro at winning people over is an ongoing interaction. It requires continuous learning, personal development, and the integration of these principles into your regular routine.

All in all, persuasion is both a science and a craftsmanship. It involves understanding the human psyche, mastering compelling correspondence, building trust, and practicing ethical persuasion. To turn into a pro at winning people over, one should leave on a journey of self-discovery and continuous refinement. As you apply the principles and procedures outlined in this aide, recall that persuasion is a power for positive change when utilized with integrity, empathy, and a genuine craving to create common benefit.

Below are some of the books written by me and my team. Please support us by ordering and reading;

https://www.amazon.com/dp/B0C4FWSYHV

https://www.amazon.com/dp/B0C2ZV7FTM

https://www.amazon.com/dp/B0C7LQH4P4

https://www.amazon.com/dp/B0C87Y14GP

https://www.amazon.com/dp/B0C5RZ8L54

https://www.amazon.com/dp/B0CD64RMHQ

https://www.amazon.com/dp/B0CHJWRZ4Q

https://www.amazon.com/dp/B0CGF745W5

https://www.amazon.com/dp/B0CFG9DW4Z

Do not forget to leave a review on the site and recommend our book to others.

May your journey be loaded up with successful persuasions and meaningful connections.

WITH LOVE

Ethan Yoder

www.ingramcontent.com/pod-product-compliance
Lightning Source LLC
Chambersburg PA
CBHW070859260726

48661CB00004B/1486